Trapped by the Ice!

Trapped by the Ice!

SHACKLETON'S AMAZING ANTARCTIC ADVENTURE

Michael McCurdy

BLOOMSBURY

NEW YORK   LONDON   OXFORD   NEW DELHI   SYDNEY

To my wife, Deborah, who helped me immeasurably while we sledged through the adventure of re-creating Shackleton's true story for you.

First published in the United States of America in 1997 by Walker Books for Young Readers, an imprint of Bloomsbury Publishing Inc.
Paperback edition published in 2002
www.bloomsbury.com

Bloomsbury is a registered trademark of Bloomsbury Publishing Plc

For information about permission to reproduce selections from this book, write to Permissions, Bloomsbury Children's Books, 1385 Broadway, New York, NY, 10018
Bloomsbury books may be purchased for business or promotional use. For information on bulk purchases please contact Macmillan Corporate and Premium Sales Department at specialmarkets@macmillan.com

Library of Congress Cataloging-in-Publication Data
McCurdy, Michael.
Trapped by the ice!: Shackleton's amazing Antarctic adventure/ written and illustrated by Michael McCurdy.
p. cm.
Summary: Describes the events of the 1914 Shackleton Antarctic expedition when, after being trapped in a frozen sea for nine months, the expedition ship, the *Endurance*, was finally crushed and Shackleton and his men made the very long and perilous journey across ice and stormy seas to reach inhabited land.
ISBN 0-8027-8438-0 (hardcover).
ISBN 0-8027-8439-9 (reinforced).
1. Shackleton, Ernest Henry, Sir, 1874-1922—Journeys—Juvenile literature. 2. *Endurance* (Ship)—Juvenile literature. 3. Imperial Trans-Antarctic Expedition, 1914-1917—Juvenile literature.
[1. Imperial Trans-Antarctic Expedition, 1914-1917. 2. Shackleton, Ernest Henry, Sir, 1874-1922—Journeys. 3. *Endurance* (Ship)]
I. Title.
G850 1914 .S53M33 1997
919.9804'092—dc21   97-6976
ISBN 0-8027-7633-7   CIP
                                 AC

Photographs on page 40 from the Scott Polar Research Institute, Cambridge, England

Book design by Maura Fadden Rosenthal
Printed in China by RR Donnelley
Printing Company, Dongguan City, Guangdong
10 9 8

4

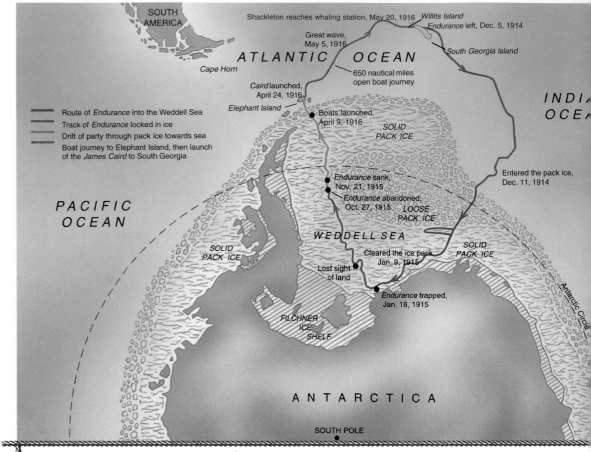

Author's Note

Sir Ernest Shackleton was a national hero in England when he began his third Antarctic trip in 1914. He had been knighted for his attempt to reach the South Pole between 1907 and 1909 after coming within 100 miles of his goal, the closest anyone had come to the pole at that time. To record his 1914 expedition, Shackleton's photographer Frank Hurley shot photographs and film footage of the adventure. Hurley was able to save about 150 of the 400 stills originally taken, as well as some movie footage, which he then had to carry with him for hundreds of miles. Many members of the crew also kept journals to record the events of the journey, which have provided me with the actual dates and details of the mishaps and highlights of their two-year ordeal. Shackleton's own book recounting the ill-fated expedition, *South*, was published in 1919.

Foreword

IN 1914, SIR ERNEST SHACKLETON (1874–1922) sailed from England on his third Antarctic expedition. Since Roald Amundsen had reached the pole in 1911, Shackleton had longed to be the first to cross the polar ice cap. After the crossing, he planned to join up with the second half of the expedition, stationed at McMurdo Sound, hundreds of miles away.

Soon after leaving South Georgia Island in the South Atlantic Ocean, Shackleton's ship, the *Endurance*, entered the ice pack of the Weddell Sea. When the ship had almost reached land, it became trapped in the ice and was carried northward by the current, away from land.

The adventure, lasting two years, is one of the most remarkable true-life survival stories on record. I hope that you are inspired to read more about what happened to Sir Ernest Shackleton and his brave men in the Antarctic during a time when there were no radios with which to call for help, no airplanes available to drop supplies and food, and no high-tech clothing to block out the cold. Shackleton and his crew went through incredible hardship and danger, never knowing from one day to the next whether any of them would survive the worst weather and the roughest seas on the globe.

October 27, 1915

$\mathcal{T}$he *Endurance* was trapped. Giant blocks of ice were slowly crushing her sides. From the deck, Sir Ernest Shackleton looked at the snow and ice that spread to the horizon. Ten months before, all he had wanted was to be the first person to cross the South Pole's ice cap. Now his only concern was for his men. What would happen to them—and how much longer did the ship have before it broke apart? The *Endurance* was leaking badly. Shack could not delay.

Shack ordered his crew off the *Endurance* and camp was set up on the frozen Weddell Sea. Tools, tents, scrap lumber for firewood, sleeping bags, and what little food rations and clothing the men had left were saved from their ship, along with three lifeboats in case they ever reached open water. The *Endurance* was a sad sight now, a useless hulk lying on its side. For months she had been the crew's home. Now they would have to get used to life on the ice—stranded hundreds of miles from the nearest land.

November 21, 1915

Almost one month later, the sound of crushing wood startled the men. It was what they had feared. Turning toward the ship's wreckage, they saw her stern rise slowly in the air, tremble, and slip quickly beneath the ice. Minutes later, the hole had frozen up over the ship. She was gone forever, swallowed by the Weddell Sea. Shack talked with the ship's skipper, Frank Worsley, and his next-in-command, Frankie Wild. Among them, they would have to decide what to do next.

Executing their plan would be difficult. By pulling the lifeboats, loaded with supplies, they would try to cross the barren ice to open water. If they made it, they would use the three boats to reach the nearest land. Shack studied the unending snow and ice ahead of him. Was it possible? Each boat was mounted on a sledge. Harnessed like horses, the men pulled, one boat at a time. Pulling 2,000-pound loads was hard work. Soon everybody was so tired and sore that no one could pull anymore. The crew would have to wait for the ice, moved by the sea's current, to carry them north to open water.

Over the next few months, food was always a concern, and it was Tom Orde-Lees's job to find it. Penguins and seals were growing scarce. To find meat to eat, hunters had to go farther away. This was dangerous. Once, when Tom was skiing back to camp, a monstrous head burst from the ice. A giant sea leopard lunged at Tom, only to slip quickly back into the dark water, stalking Tom from below, as sea leopards do when they hunt penguins. Tom tripped and fell. The huge animal lunged again, this time springing out of the water and right onto the ice. Back on his feet, Tom tried to get away. He cried for help, and Frankie Wild rushed over from camp carrying a rifle. The sea leopard now charged Frankie, who dropped calmly to one knee, took careful aim, and fired three shots. The sea leopard fell dead. There was plenty to eat for days afterward!

15

April 8, 1916

The men smelled terrible. During their five and a half months on the ice they hadn't had a bath. Clothes were greasy and worn thin, and they rubbed against the men's skin, causing painful sores. Hands were cracked from the cold and wind, and hunger sapped everyone's strength. By now, the ice floes were breaking up into smaller and smaller pieces all around the men as they drifted closer to the edge of the polar sea. Shack thought it was a good time to launch the lifeboats, rigged with small canvas sails. He knew his men could not all survive the grueling 700-mile open-boat journey to the whaling station on South Georgia Island. So he decided to try to reach Elephant Island first.

Steering around the blocks of ice was hard. The boats bumped into ice floes—or crashed into icebergs. As night fell, the boats were pulled up onto a big floe and the tents were raised. But sleeping was difficult with damp bags and blankets, and with noisy killer whales circling around.

One night, Shack suddenly felt something was wrong. He shook Frankie, and they crawled out of their tent for a look. A huge wave smacked headlong into the floe with a great thud, and the floe began to split into two pieces. The crack was headed straight toward Tent Number 4! Then Shack heard a splash. Looking into the crevasse, he saw a wriggling shape below in the dark water. It was a sleeping bag—with Ernie Holness inside! Shack acted quickly. Reaching down, he pulled the soggy bag out of the water with one mighty jerk. And just in time, too— within seconds the two great blocks of ice crashed back together.

Finally, the men reached open water. The savage sea slammed furiously into the three little boats—called the *James Caird*, the *Dudley Docker*, and the *Stancomb Wills*. Tall waves lifted them up and down like a roller coaster. Blinding sea spray blew into the men's faces. Most of them became seasick. Worst of all, they were very thirsty, because seawater had spoiled the fresh-water. The men's tongues had swelled so much from dehydration they could hardly swallow. Shack had his men suck on frozen seal meat to quench their thirst. They *had* to make land. They had to get to Elephant Island!

April 15, 1916

After an exhausting week battling the sea, the men nearly lost all hope. Big Tom Crean tried to cheer the men with a song, but nothing worked. Finally, something appeared in the distance. Shack called across to Frank Worsley in the *Dudley Docker*, "There she is, Skipper!" It was land. It was Elephant Island at last. It looked terribly barren, with jagged 3,500-foot peaks rising right up out of the sea, yet it was the only choice the men had.

23

April 24, 1916

Elephant Island was nothing but rock, ice, snow—and wind. Tents were pitched but quickly blew away. Without resting, Shack planned his departure for South Georgia Island. There he would try to get help. Twenty-two men would stay behind while Shack and a crew braved the 700-mile journey in the worst winter seas on earth. The five ablest men were picked: Frank Worsley; Big Tom Crean; the carpenter, Chippy McNeish; and two seamen, Tim McCarthy and John Vincent. With frozen fingers and a few tools, Chippy prepared the *Caird* for the rough journey ahead. Only nine days after the men had first sighted the deserted island, Shack and his crew of five were on open water once again.

For the men who stayed behind, permanent shelter was now needed or they would freeze to death. Frankie Wild had the men turn the two remaining boats upside down, side by side. Then the boats were covered with canvas and a cookstove was put inside. The hut was dark and cramped, lit only by a burning wick. And something happened that the men had not expected: heat from their bodies and the stove melted the ice under them as well as piles of frozen bird droppings left for years by the frigate birds and penguins. The smell was terrible! Day after day the men looked toward the sea, wondering if Shack would make it back to rescue them. How long would they be left here? Was Shack all right?

May 5, 1916

The *Caird* made her way through the storm-tossed seas, while Shack and his men drank rancid seal oil to prevent seasickness. The ocean swelled and hissed and broke over the small boat as the men worried about the terrible graybeards found in these waters. Graybeards are monstrous waves that come quietly and quickly, threatening everything in their path. The men had to battle to keep the boat free of ice, because any added weight might sink the *Caird*. Suddenly, Shack screamed from the tiller. The men turned around to face the biggest wave they had ever seen. It was a graybeard! The boat shuddered on impact as the mountain of water spun it around like a top. Water filled the *Caird* while the men bailed furiously. Jagged rocks in her hull, which Chippy had used to keep the boat from capsizing, saved the day.

May 10, 1916

Finally, after seventeen grueling days at sea, young McCarthy shouted, "Land ho!" South Georgia Island lay dimly ahead. The whaling station was on the other side of the island, but the men had to land *now* or die. Their freshwater was gone, and they were too weak to battle the sea to the other side of the island. While the men planned their landing attempt, they were hit by the worst hurricane they had ever encountered. For nine terrible hours they fought to keep afloat. Miraculously, just as things looked hopeless, the sea calmed enough to allow the *Caird* to land safely on the rocky beach of Haakon Bay.

31

The men landed near a small cave with a freshwater spring nearby. The cave would become a temporary home for John Vincent and Chippy McNeish. Both had suffered too much on the voyage and could not survive the long hike across the island to the whaling station. Tim McCarthy stayed behind to take care of the two sick men. Fortunately, water for drinking, wood from old shipwrecks for fire, and albatross eggs and seals to eat meant those who stayed behind would be all right while waiting for their rescue. But Shack, Big Tom, and Skipper Worsley would have to climb over a series of jagged ridges that cut the island in half like a saw blade. All they could carry was a little Primus stove, fuel for six meals, fifty feet of rope, and an ice ax. Their only food consisted of biscuits and light rations that hung in socks around their necks. On their eighth day ashore, May 18, it was time to set off on the most dangerous climb they had ever attempted.

33

Three times the men struggled up mountains, only to find that the terrain was impassable on the other side. The men stopped only to eat a soup called "hoosh," to nibble on stale biscuits, or to nap five minutes, with each man taking a turn awake so that there would be someone to wake the others. On and on the exhausted men hiked. From one mountain summit they saw that night was coming fast. Being caught on a peak at night meant certain death. They had to make a dangerous gamble. Shack assembled a makeshift toboggan from the coiled-up rope and the men slid 1,500 feet down the mountain in one big slide. Despite the perilous landing, they couldn't help but laugh with relief after they had crashed, unhurt, into a large snowbank.

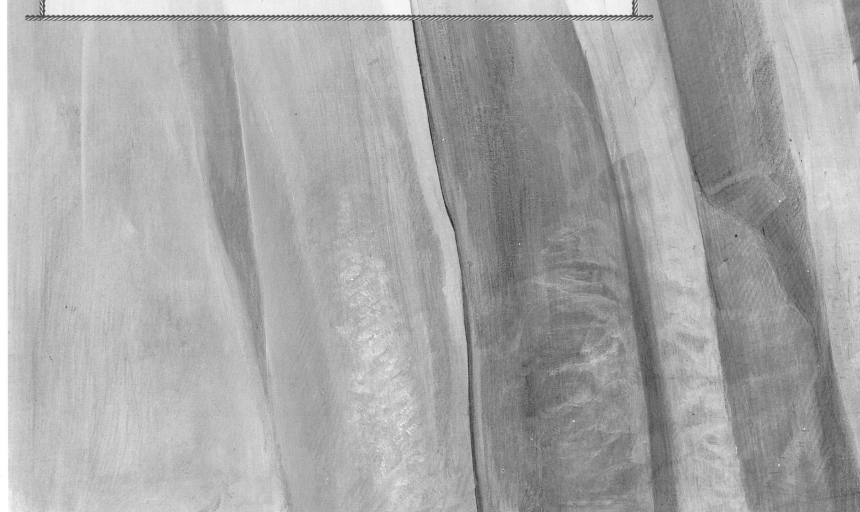

The men had survived the long slide, but danger still lay ahead. They had been hiking for more than thirty hours now without sleep. Finally, all three heard the sound of a far-off whistle. Was it the whaling station? They climbed a ridge and looked down. Yes, there it was! Two whale-catchers were docked at the pier. From this distance, the men at the station were the size of insects. Shack fought against being too reckless. The three still had to lower themselves down a thirty-foot water-fall by hanging on to their rope and swinging through the icy torrents. At last, the ragged explorers stumbled toward the station. They had done it!

4 p.m. May 20, 1916

Thoralf Sørlle, the manager of the whaling station, heard a knock outside his office and opened the door. He looked hard at the ragged clothes and blackened faces of the men who stood before him. "Do I know you?" he asked.

"I'm Shackleton," came the reply. Tears welled up in Sørlle's eyes as he recognized his old friend's voice.

The three explorers received a hero's welcome from the whaling crew. The whalers knew that no one had ever done what Shack had accomplished. The next day, Skipper Worsley took a boat and picked up McCarthy, Vincent, and McNeish while Shack began preparations for the Elephant Island rescue. It would take more than three months—and four attempts—to break through the winter pack ice and save the stranded men. But Shack finally did it—and without any loss of life. The men were glad to have a ship's deck once again under their feet. Finally, they were going home!

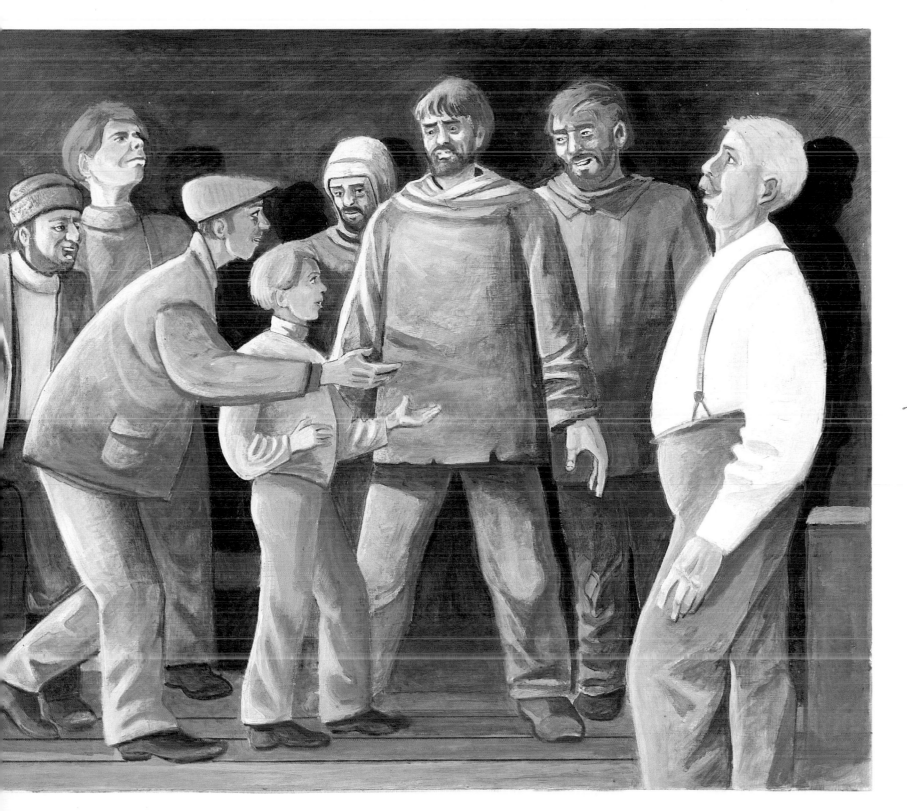

39

Afterword

What happened to Shack and the rest of the men after the expedition and their rescue from Elephant Island? Many of the men, including Big Tom Crean, joined the British military and fought in World War I, where most served on navy minesweepers. The always cheerful Tim McCarthy, who was with Shack in the open-boat journey, was killed at his gun in the English Channel. Frankie Wild was sent to the North Russian front, where he won high praise. He died in South Africa in 1938. New Zealander Frank Worsley, known to his navy mates as "Depth-Charge Bill," was the captain of two ships in World War I and was skilled at destroying German submarines. He died in 1943.

Shack toured the United States lecturing about his adventures. Then, in 1919, he went to northern Russia as part of an American mission that hoped to put down the Russian Revolution. Back in England, Shack lectured to raise money for a fourth trip to the Antarctic. Sailing on the *Quest* in September 1921, with Frankie Wild, Frank Worsley, and a handful of others from the *Endurance* expedition, he reached Rio de Janeiro in Brazil. There Shack had a massive heart attack. He refused to be examined and appeared to recover. The ship sailed on to South Georgia Island, where he saw many of his old haunts. But on January 5, 1922, Shack had another heart attack and died. He is buried under a big pile of stones on a windswept hill on South Georgia Island.

Sir Ernest Shackleton

Frank Wild

Tom Crean

Frank Worsley

Bibliography

Huntford, Roland. *Shackleton*. New York: Atheneum, 1986.

Lansing, Alfred. *Endurance: Shackleton's Incredible Voyage*. New York: Carroll and Graf Publishers, Inc., 1986.

Shackleton, Sir Ernest. *South: The Story of Shackleton's Last Expedition, 1914–17*. Edited by Peter King. North Pomfret: Trafalgar Square Publishing, 1999.

Worsley, F. A. *Shackleton's Boat Journey*. New York: W. W. Norton & Company, 1977.

Index

The year is 1914 and Sir Ernest Shackleton is determined to find adventure and fame.
His goal: to be the first to cross the Southern polar cap. What he encounters instead is a sea of ice that crushes his ship, the *Endurance*, and strands Shackleton and his crew in one of the harshest regions on the planet. It will take two hard years for Shackleton to lead his men across the frigid ice pack, through hundreds of miles of treacherous seas, and up and over a series of mountain ranges to reach help.

Miraculous but true, here is one of the most amazing survival stories on record, dashingly told by Michael McCurdy, who debuts a striking illustration style with this taut telling.

"Michael McCurdy's plain-spoken text and understated pale palette of blues, lavenders, and greens suit his story. . . . McCurdy captures not only the elemental fears but the daily grubbiness of the adventure."
—*The New York Times Book Review*

"Clear and laced with excellent detail . . . McCurdy's galvanizing enthusiasm comes across on every page."
—*Kirkus Reviews*

"The picture-book format, with its short, dated entries and full-page illustrations, works very well to create a page-turning, thrilling experience for readers."
—*Booklist*

has illustrated over 140 books. He has twice received *The New York Times* Ten Best Illustrated Books Award. Michael lives in the Berkshire hills of Massachusetts.

Cover design by Maura Fadden Rosenthal
Cover illustration by Michael McCurdy

BLOOMSBURY
CHILDREN'S
BOOKS

$9.99 U.S. / $10.99 CAN.
ISBN 978-0-8027-7633-4
50999
9 780802 776334

www.bloomsbury.com